My Little Book of Bedtime Prayers

Written and compiled by
Felicity Henderson

Illustrations by
Toni Goffe

A LION BOOK

Tring . Batavia . Sydney

Jesus, friend of little children

Jesus, friend of little children,
Be a friend to me;
Take my hand and ever keep me
Close to thee.

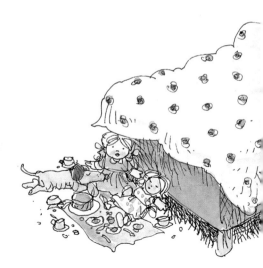

Thank you for today

Dear Jesus,
Now it's time for sleep,
I thank you for today;
For my food
And for my toys
And going out to play.

Sorry

I'm sorry I was naughty today.
Please help me to be good tomorrow.
Good night, God.

A bedtime thank you

Thank you, God, for all
the people who looked after me today.

Families

Dear God, thank you
for my family.
Please be close to all the
children who have no
families tonight.

My friend is sick

Dear God, please help
my friend to get better soon.

When I'm frightened

Dear God,
Sometimes I get frightened at night.
Please look after me tonight.

In the bathtub

Bubbles at bath-time,
Boats on the sea,
Swimming and splashing,
Now look at me!

Thank you, God, for my bath-time.

In bed

Thank you, God, for
bedtime stories, and
for my warm, cozy bed.
And thank you, too, for listening
when I say my prayers.

Mom and Dad

My mom and dad look after me.
When I am frightened they cuddle me.
Do you know something, God?
I love my mom and dad.

Time for sleep

Now it's night-time,
Now it's bedtime,
Now it's time to go to sleep.
Good night, God.

A blessing

God the Father, bless us;
God the Son, defend us;
God the Spirit, keep us
Now and evermore.

Be near me, Lord Jesus

Be near me, Lord Jesus, I ask thee to stay
Close by me for ever, and love me, I pray.
Bless all the dear children in thy tender care;
And fit us for heaven to live with thee there.

Text copyright © 1988 Lion Publishing
Illustrations copyright © 1988 Toni Goffe

Published by
Lion Publishing plc
Icknield Way, Tring, Herts, England
ISBN 0 7459 1252 4
Lion Publishing Corporation
1705 Hubbard Avenue, Batavia, Illinois 60510, USA
ISBN 0 7459 1252 4
Albatross Books Pty Ltd
PO Box 320, Sutherland, NSW 2232, Australia
ISBN 0 86760 942 7

First edition 1988

Acknowledgments
Copyright prayers as follows:
'Jesus, friend of little children'
by W. J. Mathaus, Oxford University
Press; 'God the Father, bless us'
from *Little Folded Hands,* Concordia
Publishing House Ltd

Printed and bound in Singapore